Nine Holes of Golf
Royal Cortissoz

Edited by
David Jacobsen

Published by Condor's Quill Press
Littleton, Colorado 80123
jerseygolf@comcast.net

Condor's Quill Press

a private publishing house

First Edition
ISBN: 978-0-692-17512-5

in memory of Michael Jacobsen
1955–2018
the family's first and best golfer

CONTENTS

About the Author

Royal Isaac Cortissoz was born in Brooklyn, New York, in 1869. At age fourteen, he was hired as a "menial office boy" in the famous New York architectural firm of McKim, Meade and White. The (in)famous Stanford White took Cortissoz under his wing, as he did many young men. White's protégé notably spent his off hours not carousing, but in the firm's library, reading about music and art. When the young Cortissoz let it be known that he wanted to be a journalist and write about culture, White helped him get started.

These essays first appeared in the *New York Tribune*, where Cortissoz rose to national prominence—not as a golf essayist, but as the newspaper's art editor. Over his fifty-year career in art criticism, he wrote many influential books on art and artists. These golf essays were published in book form by Charles Scribner's Sons in 1922. The *Time* magazine issue of March 10, 1930, featured Cortissoz on its cover. The article mentioned, as an aside, that the famous American art critic was "addicted to golf."

His love of golf was also noted by the Coffee House Club in New York City. A private social club founded in 1915, its membership was notoriously diverse, with a twist: it included sculptors, artists, foreigners, illustrators, authors, editors, professors, sportsmen, lawyers, actors, singers, playwrights, musicians, inventors, composers, statesmen, judges, and so on—but purposefully excluded men of finance and business.

Among the memorial plaques set into the club's long wooden dining table is one remembering Cortissoz. Under a stylized arm swinging a golf club are Latin words translated thus:

> *Here sat Royal Cortissoz,*
> *Fearless on the fairway,*
> *Cheerful in the rough.*

N.B.: While his golf essays will likely sooner or later pass (again) from wide public view, Cortissoz has 24 words that are literally written in stone. Royal Cortissoz wrote the famous epitaph engraved on the back wall of the Lincoln Memorial in Washington, D.C.

IN THIS TEMPLE
AS IN THE HEARTS OF THE PEOPLE
FOR WHOM HE SAVED THE UNION
THE MEMORY OF ABRAHAM LINCOLN
IS ENSHRINED FOREVER

A Note on the Illustrator

The cover illustration is by Tony Sarg. Anthony Frederick Sarg was born in Guatemala; lived in Germany and England; married in Cincinnati, Ohio; and rose to fame in New York City. Besides being an illustrator, a designer, and a director of several short-subject silent movies, he was a master marionettist. Sarg staged popular marionette shows at both the Chicago and New York World's Fairs (held in 1933 and 1939, respectively). He is most famously remembered today for inventing the Macy's Thanksgiving Parade floating balloons, which could be described as giant, upside-down marionettes.

It seems likely that Sarg was a golfer himself. On January 7, 1922, Rialto Productions distributed *The Original Golfer*, a silent, animated movie written and animated by Sarg. The movie is now thought to be lost. In his 1927 book, *Down the Fairway*, Bobby Jones, musing on the intersection of predestination and golf(!), wrote: "Maybe you simply play a tournament like one of Tony Sarg's marionettes, with somebody over you pulling the strings."

Concerning the Text

I have left several of the original spellings intact, such as "golf-course," "mouldy," and "dulness," as they add to the book's charm. I have also erred on the side of abundance regarding footnotes.

David Jacobsen
Littleton, Colorado

Fore!

With words as straight as an old-school, Hale Irwin 2-iron, Royal Cortissoz tells us of his golfing credentials and for whom this book is written:

> *All authoritative books about golf are written by experts. This is not an authoritative book. It is addressed to the golfer who loves the game regardless of his score.*

That this book, now almost one hundred years old, still speaks to the game of golf and those of us who play it is due in equal measure to the "ancient game" itself and to Cortissoz's skill as an essayist.

Oddly enough, if any part of this book can be termed passé, it is the first chapter—or, as he terms it, "**Hole Number One**." *On the Baldric of Porthos* is a clarion call to golfers of the early 1920s to change their drab golf attire to something more colorful. From Doug Sanders ("the peacock of the fairways"), to John Daly's "Loudmouth" line of golf pants, to Ricky Fowler's occasional orange monochrome, golf attire has long since abandoned its dreary dress.

Still, it is fun to read Cortissoz's elegantly written complaints and realize that his hoped-for revolution, *that the [fashion] revolution may sooner or later be wrought[,]*

has indeed happened. But like many revolutions, this fashion revolution has perhaps surrendered too often to its extremists.

Hole Number Two, "On Collecting Golf-Courses," records the pleasures and challenges of finding new courses to play. After stating that one's home course

> *has its virtues—above all, its familiar companionship[,]*

he notes that one's home course suffers from

> *its automatic insurance against error. Spiritually, the home course has no hazards.*

His review of his collection of courses includes interesting insights into three notable layouts: Piping Rock in Locust Valley, NY; Baltusrol in Springfield, NJ; and the National in Southampton, NY.

Hole Number Three, "On Clubs and Partners," illustrates that, in golf, 1922 was not that long ago. Surely every golfer has noticed how often the good golfer has a tidy golf bag. So did Mr. Cortissoz:

I have concluded that his [golf] status is in inverse proportion to the number of clubs which he affects.

It's equally certain that, as golfers, we have all been at least momentarily seduced by the late-night golf-club infomercial. There was no TV in 1922, but Cortissoz noted the prevalence of the

trick club, one of those specially invented marvels guaranteed to do everything short of winning the cup.

And this little nugget shows that a certain famous phrase can be dated to at least the 1920s:

Any [golf] game, they say, will serve to disclose more about a man's nature than is known even to his wife...

Additionally, a vote among golfers would pass a law that states this sentence should be read aloud by the starter to every golfer:

Neither is any spot on the course, that I ever heard of, suitable for political argument.

And finally, here is an admission from Mr. Cortissoz that all of today's golfers can agree is theirs as well:

There are times when you don't mind at all if a comrade admonishes you that attempting to kill the ball is bad golf. There are others when he persuades you that murder might make an agreeable pastime.

"On Water Hazards," **Hole Number Four**, allows Cortissoz to playfully meditate on this, the most troublesome and enigmatic of golf's hazards. He sets the familiar scene simply:

A man of brains and brawn, a hard hitter and a good player, a driver of two hundred yards and upward, is confronted by a piffling pond. He makes a mighty swing, and the ball plunges to the bottom ten yards—or less—from the shore. I have seen some beautiful players do this thing. Why?

He then provides the reader with some thoughtful, and likely helpful, answers to what is surely golf's version of the riddle of the Sphinx.

Hole Number Five starts with one of Cortissoz's best golf jokes: A golfer is having a lot of trouble getting out of a bunker. His partner/wife suggests that this passage of time might be made beneficial if she reads to him while he flails away.

That this joke begins the essay titled "On Philosophy in Golf" is typical of Cortissoz's style. In this chapter he is often insightful and occasionally profound, but such erudition never makes for turgid reading. By the end of the essay, one is likely to understand what Cortissoz means when he concludes with a paradoxical golfing truth:

> *A good shot is a good shot, no matter how it penalizes you.*

Perhaps it takes a golfer who admits to having never achieved a hole in one to muse properly on both the feat's unique nature and its universal allure. **Hole Number Six**, "On Making a Hole in One," features some of Cortissoz's best writing, including this peerless description of a hole in one he once witnessed:

> *Jim pitched a consummate ball, clean as an orchid. It landed perhaps six feet from the pin, and then, like a startled mouse, ran into the cup.*

He is at his intuitive best when he writes the following:

> *Making a hole in one, which, as I have said, has nothing to do with golf, is nevertheless one of the most sustaining stimuli known to golfers.*

He also realizes, perfectly, one of the unique features of the sport that all golfers enjoy:

> *On that emprise he and the pro are on equal terms, though on every other count they are as far apart as the poles. Is there any other game which holds out anything like the same possibility?*

And finally, has it ever been better said?

> *Making a hole in one is not an achievement at all, but an experience, such as falling in love.*

Hole Number Seven, "On Professionalism," quickly gives this warning:

> *No, reader, I don't mean what perhaps you think I do. I don't mean the difference between the sportsman who is paid for his services and the sportsman who is not. I mean a fundamental difference between two points of view, between two ways of playing the game.*

Here Cortissoz argues that "professionalism confuses art and its reward," whether that reward is money, applause, or even winning. He argues, cogently in 1922 and still so today, that when golfers pay attention to winning, they lose the spirit of the game (and often, via scoreboard watching, the tournament as well, it might be added). Cortissoz's thinking runs this way: golf is a quest for individual perfection. This perfection is impossible to attain. This quest separates golf from other sports and is the key to its lifelong allure for most every golfer.

He is certainly correct concerning perfection. Many sports allow for perfection. Hundreds of bowlers have rolled a "perfect game," more than twenty baseball pitchers have thrown a "perfect game," and scores of NFL quarterbacks have had a QBR of 158.3 for a "perfect game." Hell, even darts and snooker have had "perfect games" recorded.

To Cortissoz, the professionalism he decries is thinking that winning is the solitary point of the sport of golf. He states that it is not. And when we think about it, even PGA golfers hew to this reality. They call penalties on themselves. They give each other tips on the practice putting green. In the 1969 Ryder Cup, Jack Nicklaus conceded a missable putt to Tony Jacklin so the match could end in a draw—the first in Ryder Cup history. There was no winner except the game of golf.

To Cortissoz, who was an art critic, golf is an art. In his understanding of the game, every round played is similar to a painting—a quest for impossible personal perfection and thoroughly worth attempting every time out.

Hole Number Eight, "On the Devil in Golf," begins with an epigram worthy of Oscar Wilde:

> *If the devil is perfectly at home on a golf-course, it is doubtless because that place is so thoroughly well paved with good intentions.*

When something unlucky happens on the golf course, most golfers today lay the blame at the feet of the golf gods. Cortissoz has a darker view. Perceived "bad luck" is the work, quite simply, of the Devil.

How else to explain your shoelace breaking (at the eyelet!) right before you tee off on No. 1? All golfers will recognize the caprice of Beelzebub in these two familiar scenarios, deliciously described by Cortissoz:

> *1. As a matter of fact, there is nothing like the complete disequilibrium of all your corporeal faculties to assure you one of the best of your games.*

> *2. Get up in the morning feeling like a king, all set for a game that you have long been anticipat-*

ing. Go to the course in the most luxurious of cars. Drive off in cloudless weather, with a cherished friend, having a clear field ahead and no one to press you. It is a million dollars to a tin doughnut that you will flub your drive.

After finishing this chapter, the evidence presented makes it that much harder to remain an agnostic regarding golf's embattled theology.

In the gorgeous coffee-table book *Golf's Greatest Moments*, Robert Sidorsky collected his nominees for "the game's finest writers." In the book's first chapter, "What Makes Golf Great," it surprises no one that the novelist John Updike is included. But to the surprise of many, so is Royal Cortissoz's last chapter in *Nine Holes of Golf*. **Hole Number Nine**, titled "On Dufferdom," stands up very well in the company of Updike and the other selected writers.

This final essay is a paean to the everyday player. And just what is the nature of this region of "Dufferdom?" Cortissoz posits that the

region has, I believe, a density of population rivaling that of a Chinese slum. Only, you see, there is nothing in the least slummy about it. On the contrary, its sunny slopes are rich in elbow-room, which is used in ecstasy by happy myriads.

To Cortissoz, who happily admitted being a duffer himself, the duffer is nothing less than "the rock-ribbed foundation of golf."

The duffer is both golf's existential hero—

> *If he were to withdraw, the golf-courses of the country would infallibly bust up.*

As well as the very image of the classic hero—

> *He may top his ball, as I have said before, but he will tackle it again, and again, and yet again. His head is bloody but unbowed.*

Having finished this last chapter and this little book, most every golfer will realize that golf is at its best when played as Cortissoz said it should be played— with a fearlessness that is always cheerful.

Preface

ALL authoritative books about golf are written by experts. This is not an authoritative book. It is addressed to the golfer who loves the game regardless of his score. The author is in like case. He is by profession an art critic, on the staff of the *New York Tribune* in the columns of which journal these essays first appeared. He believes that the pursuit of beauty is as legitimate on the links as among works of painting and sculpture. Landscape is there, hills and streams and the enchantment of trees. The human body in action on the golf course is often full of beauty. And then there is the beauty of the game itself, a game dedicated to strength, skill, joy, and honor. It has its great principles, and apropos of his allusions to these, the author vehemently disclaims any pretense to offering counsels of perfection. It has simply amused him to dwell upon the ideal in golf as it might amuse an artist, painting an alp* from its base, to reflect upon the sublime possibilities of climbing the pesky thing.

---

* A high, snowcapped mountain.

On the Baldric of Porthos

I once burned a club-house to the ground. That, at all events, is what the ribald said. I had left in my locker overnight a sweater of the sublimest golden yellow, a whole sunburst in itself. Hence, they told me, the disaster. The jape*—for I suppose it may pass as a jape—is symbolical of a curious obliquity of vision prevalent in the golfing race. Many men fancy that they are affirming a certain sobriety, strength, poise, inherent in their sex, when they encase themselves in a mud-colored sweater and go abroad upon the links resembling nothing so much as a tramp escaped from a stagnant bunker. They are in error. After all, man, in his quiddity, as Lamb+ would say, is none so easy to look at. Why not do our

---

* A practical joke.
+ Presumably Charles Lamb, 19th-century English essayist.

little possible to extenuate him, to detach him from his own prosiness? This is not a light caprice. It is, I maintain, a solemn duty.

When the nineteenth century came in, some of the joy of life went out, for then color died. Painters still used it, and women, of course, kept up the cult. But man went in for wholesale renunciation. He cut his suit according to his cloth, and the only cloth he trusted was funereal black. Did he risk a blue or a gray, he was still on the safe side. And, as I have hinted, he flattered himself that in so doing he was preserving the moral order of things. To get off the stodgy key was to lapse into levity, to make himself one of Ortheris's* "peacockses," to invite the scorn of Faulconbridge for

A cocker 'd silken wanton,
Mocking the air with colors idly spread.⁺

---

* Soldier in Rudyard Kipling's *The Three Musketeers*.
⁺ Shakespeare's *King John*.

Yet the sanctions of color in masculine habiliments are to be found in no contemptible places. When Carlyle wrote his "Sartor Resartus," he extorted from the lips of Teufelsdröckh# a profound pronouncement on this subject:

> What meaning lies in Color! From the soberest drab to the high-flaming scarlet, spiritual idiosyncrasies unfold themselves in choice of Color: If the Cut be token Intellect and Talent, so does the Color be token Temper and Heart.

Precisely. Color can be, it has been on occasion, the emblem of a heroic personality, the sign and banner of a great cause. What was the oriflamme of the young romantics who rallied round Victor Hugo at the first performance of *Hernani*, nearly a hundred years ago? A red

---

Diogenes Teufelsdröckh, supposed philosopher in Carlyle's comic novel.

waistcoat, worn provocatively and proudly by Théophile Gautier*, acolyte of beauty.

But I would not leave the defense of this grand principle to the possibly fine-drawn distinctions of the philosopher or to the emotional impulses of the poet. I would assign it rather to the man of action, the man of courage, the man, in short, who wore color as boldly as he drew steel. Turn to *The Three Musketeers* and look with D'Artagnan upon Porthos+ in his glory:

> The centre of the most animated group was a musketeer of great height and haughty countenance, dressed in a costume so peculiar as to attract general attention. He did not wear the uniform cloak—which was not obligatory at that epoch of less liberty but more independence—but a cerulean blue doublet, a little faded and worn, and over this a magnificent

---

* Gautier's 19th-century literary skills included art criticism.
+ Porthos is the admitted extrovert of the three.

baldric worked in gold, which shone like water ripples in the sun. A long cloak of crimson velvet fell in graceful folds from his shoulders, disclosing in front the splendid baldric, from which was suspended a gigantic rapier.

Phoebus Apollo! What a crescendo! First cerulean blue, then gold, shining like water ripples in the sun, and finally a great sheet of crimson! And, reader, was Porthos a mystagogue of the dandiacal body, or was he a mighty man of his hands? "It is permitted to mankind, under certain restrictions, to wear white waistcoats."* White waistcoats, forsooth! One can as soon imagine Porthos contenting himself with that tepid indulgence as one can imagine him tossing off a beaker of—sarsaparilla. He was a man's man. He had the courage of his convictions. He wore what he liked. O wise and endearing Porthos!

If there is any place that cries aloud for a revival of his manly tradition, it is the golf-course,

---

* *Sartor Resartus*, again.

where grass, trees, and sky provide a background spacious enough to keep any color, no matter how plangent, well in the picture—and where there is a strong tendency to regard any old rags as providing an adequate make-up for the game. There are numerous golfers, it is true, who have a decent sense of the fitness of things. Latterly they have been adopting the English practice of playing in jackets. But everybody knows the type of golfer who is no more than Carlyle's "omnivorous Biped that wears Breeches," and they are very mouldy breeches at that. He heaves into view disheveled and deplorable. That he is amenable to reason, especially reason of an artistic nature, I gravely doubt. On the other hand, it is not unbelievable that the revolution may sooner or later be wrought. In the first place, the sweaters are available. The makers make them, and obviously they would not do so if they had no market. Here and there adventurous spirits arise willing, like Porthos, to put their conviction to the test, the conviction that to "add another hue unto the rainbow" is not, in very truth, "wasteful and ridiculous excess," but, on the contrary, one way of washing the eyes clear of ugliness and dulness.

I have observed one great golfer whom I would not hesitate to reckon of the tribe of Porthos. The only time I ever saw Bobby Jones on the links, he wore a glowing red beret. He played, of course, like a consummate artist. But he stays in my memory chiefly as a magnificent young portent, an apocalyptic cherub, whose topknot set a livelier mark upon the horizon than was ever placed there by the white plume of Navarre.* I do not know his taste in sweaters. But I like to cherish the idea that it is tinged with the aesthetic fervor I divined in his cap. Is it objected that there is nothing masculine, nothing hardy, nothing sportsmanlike in this matter of color? In the bull-ring, where the most perilous of all sports is practiced, the colors of the players are resplendent. Years ago, I saw the greatest matador in Spain, Espartero, killed in the ring at Madrid. He went to his death caparisoned as

---

* King Henry IV of France, aka "Henry of Navarre."

though for a fancy ball. The golfer, rambling along in his pastoral security, may see no reason in this for emulating the dying dolphin,

> Whom each pang imbues
> With a new color as it gasps away,
> The last still loveliest.[+]

But at least he may reasonably do something to lift himself above his present drab level and shake off his kinship with the chimney-sweep.

[+] From Lord Byron's *Childe Harold's Pilgrimage.*

On Collecting Golf-Courses

IF golf were only a game, it would not appeal to the meditative man. But it is, far more, like Platonism, a habit of mind. Hence its lure. In tennis, you are confined to one spot and exhaust yourself in acrobatic exercise like a squirrel in a cage. In baseball, you sit in the bleachers and howl. In golf, you do not loaf, not by any means, but you invite your soul.

It is one of the few adventures left in an age of prose. It is one of those pursuits in which the goal lies perpetually just over the brow of the hill, from which place it also perpetually recedes. A businessman can resolve to make a fortune— and make it. I have seen the thing done. Did you ever know a golfer who, by taking thought, could develop the game of which he dreams? Or a golfer who really wanted, once and for all, to do anything of the sort? To go after a score might seem, superficially, to ally the golfer with Jason and the Argonauts, in quest of the Golden Fleece. Actually, he is more like Sisyphus, rolling a stone up-hill, only to have it roll down again. And your true golfer watches the descent with a grin. When he's got his score, it is of no earthly use to him save as an incentive.

It is the same in the matter of golf-courses. Unimaginatively speaking, the character of a golfer's game is determined by his own course. This is a fallacy. Certain humdrum factors in a golfer's state of mind are settled when he is elected. Convenience looms large. He becomes habituated to the process of getting there. He doesn't have to carry his clubs to and fro. His locker-room presently fits him like an old coat. But the course itself only too soon takes on the quality of safety which is the bane of our modern life. The golfer learns absolutely what to avoid, a killing detriment to sport. He plays short on the second hole. In that way he keeps out of the brook and then can get on the green in three, anyway. No, the home course has its virtues—above all, its familiar companionships—but its blight is its automatic insurance against error. Spiritually, the home course has no hazards. It is in the collecting of courses that you escape this most deadening of handicaps.

The adventure begins with the invitation from your friend. Will it rain that day? If so, you may be dished out of that particular course for weeks, perhaps forever. Will you have to tote your clubs on a train, or will he throw in a car? Will it be a touring-car* or a limousine? This is important. In a touring-car, even on a windless day, your cigar ashes blow back in your face. Then there is the mystery of the locker-room. It may be perfection itself. Or you may have to improvise an entirely new expression of contentment when your host bids you stuff your dunnage into a pill-box already crowded with old

---

* A big convertible.

clothes and clubs and mouldy shoes. The best locker-room I know is at Piping Rock,[+] where you do not, as a guest, use it at all, but change in a spacious, airy room lined with broad settees, a cross between a boudoir and an Epicurean lounge. Well, you discover and inhabit that territory for a few moments and then, with the first tee, you are immediately aware of ideal golfing conditions.

The lay of the land is totally unfamiliar. Distance, despite the card or the figures on the sand box, is purely a matter of guesswork, for distance in golf is but partially dependent upon the eye; it involves feeling, where precedent plays its part. Your drive is complicated by a mixture of emotions. You hate to embarrass your host by making it too good and putting the fear of death into him at the start; nor would you humiliate him in the eyes of his watching fellow members by revealing the disability of the duffer all at once. It is a very subtle and difficult thing to strike the

---

[+] Locust Valley, NY. Very selective, private course. Think Jay Gatsby, back in the day. By Macdonald and Raynor in 1912.

happy medium off the first tee. By some fluke
you do it. You make a passable drive. Through
sheer excess of confidence your host (who, you
see, is playing on his own course!) makes a hopeless flivver.* I leave it to the recording angel to
put down your thoughts and emotions. The
point here is simply that the game is on. Everything is new and strange. The lurking dangers
are past finding out. You are tickled to death
when you find that you have conquered one.
Your host's praise is doubly sweet, for does not
your ignorance make your triumph doubly clever?

Heaven swims into your ken if the next
hole is a blind one. Orations on the part of your
host. "You'd better drive to the right. There is a
bad slope beyond that bunker. The green is just
at the foot of it, and there is an ugly pit+ to the
left. But it's a comparatively short hole. You can
easily reach it." Easily! The whole affair is dark,
mysterious, full of a delicious terror. Could any-

---

* A car or airplane that is cheap and/or in rather rundown condition.
+ Sand bunker.

thing be more thrilling? Could anything make a more powerful appeal to the spirit of adventure? The collecting of courses means, naturally, just this collecting of holes, this opening of vistas, this blithe exploration of undiscovered countries. On every properly constituted course there are at least two or three holes which are the bliss of exasperation in excelsis.

The third at Piping Rock is a good example. Item: You must get over the rough. Item: It must be a high ball, for the green is in the air. Item: Too much to the right will land you in a pit. Item: Too much to the left, ditto. Item: If you land on the green or even if you run up on it, big as it is, you can easily bounce or roll into Perdition beyond. Item: You can see the pin, yet it is virtually a blind hole.

Heard melodies are sweet,
but those unheard are sweeter.[*]

---

[*] John Keats, "Ode on a Grecian Urn."

A hole that lies in full view can be exciting enough, but the one that invokes not only a swing, but faith and instinct, is the hole that gives golf an edge. Isn't the unseen hazard the one that most potently swells your bosom—when you find your ball in it?

There used to be a wonderful hole at Baltusrol.[+] You drove from a height, over a pool placed in the immediate foreground, a nominally negligible hazard, though evidently inserted, as in the riddle, "to make it more difficult," and sometimes succeeding in that end. Then came a lot of devastating rough, and at last, beyond a trifle of fairway, the hole, set in an emerald disk entirely surrounded by a narrow belt of water. A duck[*] of a hole, tantalizing and inspiring! One could have profitably spent a whole summer playing it in hopes of a three—sustained by stories of how this or that wizard had made it in two. But the last time I played there it was out of

---

[+] Springfield, NJ. Tillinghast, 1922. Having reached this page, readers likely know of this course. (See more below.)
[*] British informal, meaning "dear" or "darling."

commission, permanently, I was told, because of some reorganization of the course.[+] I was never more shocked in my life. I have always had a great respect for the Baltusrol committee. I have been grateful when they have permitted me to divagate over their domain. A fine lot of impeccable gentlemen, I'm sure, good fellows, brilliant golfers—but cruel spoil-sports, all, if they have conclusively suppressed that most stimulating episode.

There they had a hole of holes, a hole that was romance itself, and they were tempted into sacrificing it, I dare say, by some recondite theory of "good golf." I like good golf. If I could play it, I do not doubt that my whole outlook upon life would be changed. But the artist in me would nevertheless go on mourning the water hole aforesaid.

[+] This "reorganization" was A. W. Tillinghast plowing under the "Old Course" in the process of building today's Upper and Lower Courses. The hole Cortissoz laments losing was #10, a 314-yard par-4 named "Island" on the scorecard. It was likely America's first "island hole," predating the ninth hole at Shackamaxon Country Club in Westfield, NJ (1916), the fifteenth hole at Galen Hall Golf Club in Wernersville, PA (1917), and, of course, the seventeenth hole at TPC Sawgrass (1982).

There are some enchanting holes at Orange and at Morristown. Englewood* is a beguiling course. The first hole, a decent, negotiable affair, gives you no warning at all of the difficulties at tending the take-off at the second, and these, warming as they are, leave you without the slightest hint of the awful job sitting back for you at the eighteenth. But though New Jersey has added substantially to my collection, it is on Long Island that I have found the richest treasure. To Garden City[†] I would only allude in passing—with profound respect. It is a bleakly hard course, meant for super golfers. I have made two or three holes there in par. What has happened to me on some of the others, where a peculiarly diabolical rough stretches for miles, I forbear from saying. Life would be a little more satisfactory at Garden City if the course had more, let us say, charm. Chimneys. Water-towers. They don't uplift a game.

---

* Likely Englewood GC in New Jersey, which hosted the 1909 U.S. Open. In the 1960s, construction of the NJ Turnpike Extension doomed the course. (Another reason to abhor the dreaded NJ Turnpike.)
[†] Devereaux Emmet, 1889; Walter Travis, 1906.

The National,# at Southampton, is full of charm, a glorious course, riotous in color, and with the nearness of water immensely enhancing its beauty and exhilaration. The National may be even more difficult than Garden City, but there is a curious amelioration of this in the broad character of the scheme. For one thing, it abounds in tees, for all ages, sizes, and sexes. The shortest of them gives you something to do. It has some blind holes that are masterpieces.

The finest sea-holes I know are at the Maidstone* course, over at East Hampton. There are two of them, built on the farthermost dunes. You drive literally out to sea, right into the blue, across snowy sand sprinkled with tufts of exquisite green. I say "drive." The wizard would say "pitch," the holes are so short. But that doesn't help you to evade the pits that pro-tect the greens or keep you from running up and over the ramparts that loom against the surf.

Macdonald and Raynor, 1908. Very, very exclusive.
* Reworked several times; recently by Coore & Crenshaw, 2013. Despite *Caddyshack*, Chevy Chase was allowed mem-bership in1981.

When I have got a two on one of these holes, I have felt that that made it a day.

Oaklands[‡] is a fine course, one that always seems to me a little longer than any other in the world, though I fancy it is no stronger in what they call "yardage" than a score more on the island. It has a large, spacious character. Yes, "character" is the word, where golf-courses and holes are concerned. Consider the seventh and eighth at Oaklands. The first of these is infested by a personal devil. The second is angelic, lying across the most deceptive of gulfs, provided with the most resilient of greens, and yielding, in a two, about as golden a reward as man could ask.

The most temperamental course in Christendom is the one at Great Neck[+] probably because it numbers a good many actors among its

---

[‡] Likely Oakland in Queens, NY. Died (1960) a slow death thanks to the Long Island and Clearview Expressways. (Another reason to abhor the dreaded "LIE.")

[+] Great Neck Golf and Country Club became Sound View GC and is also no longer with us.

disciples. Fully to extract from it the last drops of ecstasy one should play it with Frank Craven, Ernest Truex, and Grantland Rice, with Ring Lardner§ lending the presence of a brooding Buddha to the scene. There are no dull holes at Great Neck, and one of them is unique. I gathered that Craven had had some esoteric influence upon the devising of that hole; Hell Gate,# I think they call it. You drive off a trick tee. The pins are so placed that you think you are taking the proper stance, when, as a matter of fact, you are heading your ball almost anywhere save at the cup. No matter how you stand, you face an interminable gash in the earth filled with water, black mud, and tussocks, and you face it the long way. After sending a flight of balls into this no man's land, you think you have the stance and get a ball over. Retrieving what you have left in the gash and emerging from the tussocks looking like a disheveled Bolshevist, you discover that the

---

§ Craven and Truex were actors; Rice and Lardner were both famous writers, notably about sports.
# A narrow, dangerous tidal strait in the East River in New York City.

ball you got over is lost in a plantation several perches or furlongs off the course. So you stroll on to the green and learn that everybody else has a three or thereabouts. Then they lead you to the next tee and point to the green, up a short hill, short but as steep as the side of a bonded warehouse. This is where Ring Lardner comes in. You look at his calmness, and you are fortified. There is everything in calm when you are collecting golf-courses. Unless you have serenity, it is better to stick to the home course.

On Clubs and Partners

IF a man is known by the company he keeps, his status as a golfer is surely to be told from the clubs he carries or stores in his locker. After much careful observation, I have concluded that his status is in inverse proportion to the number of clubs which he affects. In the very beginning, a rather redundant battery may mean nothing but a pardonable ardor. What more natural than that he who has just entered the blissful land of golf, that delectable valley of Avilion, "Where falls not hail or rain or any snow, / Nor ever wind blows loudly,"* should arm himself with every implement that the game allows? But the test comes a little later, with that stage of struggle at which you oscillate between respect

---

* Alfred, Lord Tennyson, *Morte d'Arthur*.

for an art and "a proper conceit of oneself." It ought to be easy enough to admit that there is something the matter with your swing. But it is ever so much easier to say: "There must be something the matter with this club." Hence, the enrichment of club-makers and the tendency toward discrimination amongst caddies. The latter are not necessarily lazy when they balk at some bags. They simply shrink from being beasts of burden, toting a small forest of clubs up hill and down dale. In the preface to Albrecht Dürer's *Four Books of Human Proportions* there is a story of his meeting with Giovanni Bellini in Italy.* "I want you," said the Venetian, "to make me a present of one of the brushes with which you draw hairs . . . with which you draw several hairs with one stroke; they must be rather spread out and more divided, otherwise in a long sweep such regularity of curvature and distance could not be preserved." Durer produced a handful of his ordinary brushes, the same as those that Bellini himself employed. "I use no others than

---

* Dürer (1421-1578) and Bellini (1430-1516) were both artists during the Renaissance.

these," he said, "and to prove it, you may watch me," proceeding thereupon to excite his friend's wonderment by the sheer perfection of his draftsmanship. I thought of this the other day when I watched the ineffable tee shots of Mitchell and Duncan.[+] Those heroes of the game were not wearing anything recondite in the way of clubs. They merely knew how to drive a ball out of sight. No doubt the feel of an accustomed driver is as important to a long-hitting player as the feel of his own violin is to a musician. The "favorite club" is obviously a legitimate thing. But there are favorites of another kind, the clubs that are just so many concessions to a weakness or to arbitrary theory. I know a driver who repeatedly gets a good iron shot off the tee and eschews wood because it usually heaves his ball a parasang[*] or two off the course. He thinks, therefore, that there is something talismanic about iron. There, I am convinced, he deceives

---

[+] Abe Mitchell and George Duncan were both British professional golfers.
[*] A historical Iranian unit of distance traveled; similar to a "league."

himself. He is a victim of the "favorite-club" delusion. It's no use. Science won't make things any easier for the golfer. I have long had in my bag a trick club, one of those specially invented marvels guaranteed to do everything short of winning the cup. Particularly was it supposed to aid in the useful process of "lifting the ball." It did that just enough for it to become my inseparable club. But there befell a day when, in the frenzy that goes with trying to play the National at Southampton, I hit something other than the ball, and during the luncheon-hour I left the club in the shop to be put in order. The wise repairer thought that that meant eliminating the trick feature, and I started out on the afternoon round mourning an irreparable loss. Only, as it happened, now that the club had been made normal, it worked better than ever! The men in the shops, I fancy, could throw some lurid light on this whole question. How many drivers have they not been asked to "loft just a little bit more"—as though that had anything to do with it.

There is a deadly fascination about the pet club. Why, I once knew a man who found his happiness in a cleek,* and he could make it mind, too. Another player recurs to me who maintained that the only legitimate club in a bunker—save when you were buried in a heel print—was a putter, and he forthwith showed that he was right. Everybody knows the golfer who wouldn't be caught dead pitching his ball onto the green with a mashie.[+] He always runs it up with a jigger.[#] After all, why not? I've never been able to see why not—until I've seen a master pitch up crisp and bold.

> Then felt I like some watcher of the skies
> When a new planet swims into his ken.[±]

The precious ball has risen as though there were some truly controlling force behind it; it has described a curve flawless in itself and in

---

[*] A metal-headed club with a bit of loft, similar to a modern 1- or 2-iron.
[+] Similar to today's 5- or 6-iron.
[#] Similar to a modern chipper.
[±] John Keats, "On First Looking into Chapman's Homer."

direction; it has fallen all but dead upon the green, and it has lain confidently in the immediate neighborhood of the hole. Seeking a club that will automatically do that for you is very like trying to pull yourself up by your boot-straps. When the bulge-faced drivers bulged in not so long ago, they were highly commended by a friend of mine who waved one exultingly on the first tee, with gay threats of giving the ball a record-breaking ride. There was to be no more hooking, no more slicing. Here was a club that made par safe for the humblest. Then he popped his ball into a shrub about twenty yards to the right. It was a perfect lesson, but not conclusive. I had to get one myself and find my own shrub before the moral of the bulged face really went home. That is, perhaps, the only way in which to absorb the fact that it is not the club that does the business but the swing behind the club—the only way, save the best way of all, which is to take a good trouncing from the man who goes around with, say, three clubs.

A certain parallel may be drawn between clubs and companions. The game involves har-

monious adaptation to both. If there is excite-
ment in a new club, so there is in an antagonist
you have never met before. A foursome of previ-
ously unrelated elements is as good as a play.
Everybody's first drive arouses expectation, in
which curiosity and emotions of complacency or
anxiety are nicely intermingled. And the situation is the more amusing because first drives are
not by any means invariably prophetic. Then it
remains to be seen whether all four have a reasonable pace or if there is a citizen in the group
who moves with Johnsonian* deliberation. Getting into trouble is a practically universal foible.
And getting out of it is an affair in which the
margin for the expression of individuality is infi-
nite. The phase that is actually poignant comes,
however, with the first putting-green.

I wonder if any of the ceremonial oracles
in golf have ever plotted out a definitive rule for
the placing of players on the putting-green. The
precedence off the tee, down steps, over bridges,

---

* Samuel Johnson, eighteenth-century writer of wit and much
else.

and so on, of the man who has the honor, has been settled. There ought to be as rigid a technic for the green, one determining positions, as for a minuet. That is where golf etiquette culminates. That is where you find out if a man has practised the immobility of a pillar of salt, or if he has been born to wear creaky shoes, or if he is unaware of the circumstance that a solid body casts a shadow. Is there a rule against totting up the score on the green? There might well be one. It would protect a lot of us against our besetting sin.

You learn players as you learn clubs. Sooner or later you know the ones with whose potentialities you can rest on happy terms. Any game, they say, will serve to disclose more about a man's nature than is known even to his wife; and golf, which is carried on over acres, is probably the most intimate and revealing of them all. It is curious to observe the tenacity of its affections. I have mentioned the dramatic charm, a charm by itself, of the game played with new companions. It is priceless, because such a game holds the factors of mystery and surprise, which mean so much to your devoted golfer. But there is probably no course in the United States on which the majority of the players have not their long-established partners and opponents. It is not a matter of propinquity alone. Mankind may occasionally marry on that hypothesis,* but golf requires something more. Golf is a matter of pure friendship—one reason more for designating it the king of games. The ideal partner is not determined for you by the caliber of his game or of your own. It is altogether a question of conversation—in a game which permits little—and of mutual sympathies and tastes. These can be put into no formula, yet on one point it is safe to dogmatize: The spirit of the game is sufficiently combative, but it is at bottom serene and measured. If your partner doesn't realize this, you are lost.

---

* Cortissoz speaks from experience here. Some 25 years earlier he had married Ellen MacKay Hutchinson, a literary editor who also worked at the *Tribune.*

The golfer who may be the life of the locker-room is hopeless on the links if he carries too much of his vivacity there. The putting-green is no place for pranks, even though they be no more than verbal. Neither is any spot on the course, that I ever heard of, suitable for political argument. It is axiomatic that any conversational episode, to be fitted to the game, must have, following Aristotle, a beginning, a middle, and an end, all negotiable in something well under two minutes. The joke that has to be carried over from one shot to the next is a contradiction in terms. It is not a joke. It is a tactless distraction. A mood of reverie is the right mood for golf. This lets beauty in, which is one of the vitalizing forces in the game. Nature is always worth contemplation. So are some shots.

How far the golfer should be laid open to analytical comment upon his game is a delicate and debatable question. There is occasionally solace in an opponent's criticism. "You lifted your head that time." It is a piece of information that almost consoles for a topped ball. At least, you know therefrom what is happening to your game. But where the deeper horrors of that game are concerned the lasting value of good counsel depends profoundly upon the moment, upon the state of your temper, upon your score for the preceding hole, upon any number of things. There are times when you don't mind at all if a comrade admonishes you that attempting to kill the ball is bad golf. There are others when he persuades you that murder might make an agreeable pastime.

On Water Ḥazards

THERE is a golf-course just south of Lake George, belonging to the Glens Falls Country Club, which offers the player such a test as I have not encountered anywhere else in explorations over from thirty to forty courses. It begins the game with its principal water hazard staring one in the face at the edge of the first tee.* To be sure, it is not a hazard of prodigious width; it is well under a hundred yards. But a bowl of water only a few yards across has been known to play havoc with the nerves of the kind of golfer who "looks on tempests and is never shaken."+ Is there any more familiar spectacle in golf? A man of brains and brawn, a hard hitter and a good player, a driver of two hundred yards and up-

---

* This first hole still plays over this "bowl of water." Donald Ross was the architect for Glens Falls Country Club, 1912.
+ Shakespeare's Sonnet 116, "Let Me Not to the Marriage of True Minds."

ward, is confronted by a piffling pond. He makes a mighty swing and the ball plunges to the bottom ten yards—or less—from the shore. I have seen some beautiful players do this thing. Why?

If the literature on the subject is small, it is, I suppose, partly because there is so much profanity connected with it. Men never swear at a ball half so hard or so profusely as when it has taken a bath and added implacably a stroke to the score. Then, too, the waterless condition of the average course accounts in a measure for the nominally obscure status of the water hazard in the annals of golf. Some players, freed by happy accident in their local course from the negotiation of brooks, pools, streams, estuaries, ponds, lakes, and what not, live and die under the impression that the worst thing you can get into is a bunker or a pit. Pathetic fallacy! Out of the most evil trap or the most tenacious rough in the land you may, by good luck, emerge with next to no penalty, with no more than a certain paring down of distance. I have seen Cyril Tolley* get incredibly far out of eel-grass high enough, dense enough, and tangled enough to have embarrassed an eel. He lifted the ball with a niblick+ as easily as you would pick a cherry out of a basket. But a ball in the water would cost even Tolley or Sarazen# a stroke. Tribulations in the rough and traps are only minor sorrows. Deviation into a water hazard is another matter altogether.

It is mental, we are told with finality, as though that settled the business. But its psychology goes deeper. The hazard at Glens Falls provokes some suggestive reflections. Its whole significance, obviously, is that you must drive it at once, without any preparation, without any warming up. It takes you by the throat, on your merits. If you've got any golf in you, it must show then and there. "Bravo!" you cry. "What a

---

* British amateur golf champion.
+ Similar to today's 9-iron or wedge.
# Gene Sarazen, winner of seven major championships from 1922-1935.

clever committee!" Too clever by half. The tee faces an arm of the lake. As you walk around the water to reach it, you perceive, just to the right, the eighteenth green. The tee for that is near the club-house, and your mashie pitch is only across one hundred and twenty-five yards, spanning a much shorter distance over the lake itself, which is here at its narrowest stretch. All you have to do is to play the eighteenth hole first, and you are lured to do that since it will save a little walk at the fatigued end of your round. Incidentally, you see, too, you have a preliminary and easy try at the lake. You get your warming up and the demon of the water hazard is exorcised. I don't know whether or not the committee figured this all out, but the fact remains that even at Glens Falls, where the water hazard was to put the golfer absolutely on his mettle, the upshot of this valiant planning left a loophole for evasion.

Mental fiddlesticks! The reactions, so to say, associated with the water hazard are profounder, more searching. They are allied with the bases of a man's moral nature. And it is a very curious thing that in the habits and customs of the game there has been for years a factor insidiously and speciously sapping at the very central strong hold of golfing character. I refer to the floater.* Who invented it? Who first insinuatingly handed the golfer this treacherous aid to his weakness, this compromise with his essential purpose, this emblem of his dufferish state? He ought to wear a name more forbidding than Bogey. Of course, he would plead economic wisdom. A floater costs less than a sinker, and, besides, it is frequently retrievable. But, as it floats, it proclaims the duffer's shame. There is only one slogan for the golfer at a water hazard. The Marquis of Montrose+ wrote it:

> He either fears his fate too much,
> Or his deserts are small,
> Who fears to put it to the touch
> To gain or lose it all.

---

* "Floaters" are a type of golf ball used today at driving ranges with ponds and at backyard swimming-pool golf games.
+ 17th century Scottish soldier and poet.

Moreover, there is always retribution wait-
ing at the water hazard, a rebuke for pusillani-
mous precaution. You try a floater. Very well.
Promptly you prove that it does not belie its
name. You try another. "Boy, that one is over
there by the rushes." There are no more in the
bag, so you try a sinker. Oh, miracle! It flies over,
far beyond the shore. "Why didn't I try that in
the first place," you wonder. Why wonder? If
you had used the sinker in the first place, you
would probably have gone over. The more precious the ball the surer the chance, if only because the player will take a little more pains in
driving such a ball—a sordid reason, if you like,
but one at any rate tending to coerce a player
into keeping his eye where it belongs. The wise
golfer, who is matching not only his skill but his
sportsmanship against the handicaps of the
game, will take out only one ball when he meets
a deadly water hazard. That will be his best and
newest sinker. If he gets over, his satisfaction will
be doubled. If he fails, he will have learned that
lesson so often commended to us—"To give till it
hurts." If I had any influence over the solons

who settle the laws of golf, I would get them to abolish the floater as an incentive to trifling with the discipline of the game. For one thing, I wouldn't then be able to buy any floaters any more.

While I was about it, I would also beg the arbiters of golfing destiny to exact on all courses an increase in the number and scope of water hazards. When there isn't one on the spot it should be made, though the line should be drawn at such a cement basin as once disfigured a certain distinguished course not a thousand miles from New York. There was something factitious about that terrible tub, and it was ugliness itself besides. The right art is disclosed, of course, in making the most of a natural hazard. There is a priceless example on the Ekwanok* course at Manchester. It occurs on the third hole, where it protects the green. The approach from any distance at all is wickedly deceptive, for until you are very near you cannot see how the land slopes just enough to woo even a gently rolling ball to

---

* 1900, by Walter Travis, in Manchester, VT.

disaster. Only a mashie stroke calculated to a nicety will lay the ball on the green. The least slackening will let the ball roll in. The water when I last saw it was hardly an inch deep. But the banks are very high, and on the green side so near to the vertical as to make the job like that of urging a ball straight up the side of a house. Once in that awful fix there is nothing to do but bind your hair in blue and take up the plaint of Swift's starling. Stockbridge** has a water hazard as exasperating as it is odd and with an ingenious moral twist. You drive almost with the stream along its length, save for the necessary slant to reach the farther shore. The test lies in the angle you adopt; you can make the drive long or short to suit yourself. You can play golf, or you can play safe.

It is human to play safe, and its economical possibilities offer an inducement not to be lightly condemned. But as I have more than once endeavored to point out in these musings,

---

** In Stockbridge, MA. Founded in 1895, a pioneer of America's "summer courses," its original layout gradually increased until it reached eighteen holes in 1901.

the genius of golf lies in its pure idealism, its spur in the struggle after perfection. Your true water hazard is a great call to courage, to the high spirit of the game. There are brook-holes at Scarsdale,* for example, which are very charming, but each one of them is vitiated by the temptation to compromise. They can all be conquered by playing safe. The broad lake, going out or coming in, offers no alternative—you must drive across or confess yourself beaten. The brook-holes, in their turn, may have their virtue. To play a ball out of one of them with a niblick, thereby covering yourself from head to foot with mud and water, is no slight sacrifice of comfort to ambition. But to take your own golfing measure you must address your ball before an indubitably sizable body of water; you must set your argosy+ really upon "the inconstant billows dancing."#

---

* 1898, W. Dunn, and 1920s, A. W. Tillinghast; in Hartsdale, NY.
+ A large ship with precious cargo.
# Shakespeare, *Henry V.*

On Philosophy in Golf

IT happened at Walton Heath,[*] in England. A member of Parliament was in a bunker, with a niblick, golfing. His wife was standing nearby, patiently observing him, and presently she said: "Charles, shall I read to you while you do that?" Obviously he needed something to sustain him in a crisis of this sort, one in which insult was added to injury. And as obviously he had it, for the story does not add that he either killed the lady or gave up the game. Opinions may differ as to just what pulled him through. One analyst of the episode might be content with calling the M. P. a good sportsman. Another

---

[*] In Surrey, England; 1903, by Herbert Fowler. The course has been long associated with English kings and politicians, from Edward VIII to Winston Churchill.

might possibly assert that he was upheld by an incurable enthusiasm.

I maintain simply that he was a philosopher. There is a philosophy of golf, which is not explained by ardor or sportsmanship. Indeed, I am not sure but that it is by some subtle paradox antithetical to sportsmanship, though frequently coexistent with it in the selfsame golfing soul. About true sportsmanship, I take it, there is something chivalrous. From respect for an antagonist you rise into admiration for him. Sportsmanship without generosity is a contradiction in terms. When you have just lost a hole and your opponent takes the honor at the next tee, we will assume that he hits out a perfectly sweet, clean ball, straight down the course, for a good two hundred yards. We will assume also that you rejoice with him in his drive. Surely that is part of the game. But if he fluffs it into the rough, about ten yards off, wouldn't it take a fearful lot of assumption to credit you with immeasurable sorrow?

It is curious how, in such a moment, philosophy creeps in. You say, "Hard luck," of course. There are always the decencies to be observed. But you proceed to make your own drive in a mood of resignation, which develops into something like complacency if by good luck you get beyond the rough. And are you downhearted if, by any bad luck, you fluff it, too? Not at all. For are not you and your dear friend even off the tee?

It all comes back to the law of compensation. The golfer, no matter how much he may esteem himself, is after all only a child at play, and, like a child, what his heart craves is consolation. When Wilkins minor, aged three, silver mug in hand, falls off a rug and abrades his damask cheek, all he requires is that Mummy shall rush to him "to kiss the spot and make it well." When Wilkins major, aged thirty-three, going strong on his game and hopeful of a mug with the date of a tournament scratched upon it, falls off his drive, all that is needed to keep the glow upon his brazen cheek is for the enemy to slice into a pit—or in some way to keep the thing "all square." I have observed the operation of this philosophical instinct upon several occasions.

Once, for example, I had the pleasure (not at all unfamiliar) of a match with a golfer exceedingly my superior. We ding-donged along for a number of holes with no salient incidents. He merely took the honor and kept it until we came to one of the longest holes on the course, with the trickiest of all the greens. I don't know what accounted for the adequacy of my wooden shots, my successful use of the midiron, or the approach that took me over a nasty obstacle onto the green, with a long putt to contemplate. Least of all can I account for the putt itself, which sank the ball for a win. It took me a minute to come to, and, when I was to, I found I hadn't budged. I measured that putt, foot by foot, and when the job was done, I said to my opponent: "Listen, this is going down in my memoirs as my forty-foot putt." He swallowed hard for a moment and then quoth he gravely: "But see here, old chap, your foot isn't twelve inches long." You remark how philosophy slipped in to kiss his cheek and make it well.

I have known this consolatory movement of the golfing mind to lift a man above positive disaster. It was in a threesome this time, the third member of which fairly looped the loop around his companions. But at the seventeenth tee fortune smiled upon us. My partner drove a most edifying ball, over the rough, beyond the bunker, a good bit up the fairway on the hill. It must have inspired me, for I contrived, somehow, to follow suit. Then smote he the ball, our Master, a super wallop, leagues over the bunker. Only it was sliced tragically off the course, into rough sprinkled with boulders, which, to make matters worse, were disposed in front of a stone wall running at right angles to the fairway. You figure our anguish, comfortably set for the next move and obliged to regard a comrade in such appalling distress. For him to get out of his mess was job enough. For him to gain any distance to speak of in the process was merely impossible. The only thing to do was to "play safe" back onto the fairway, at the sacrifice of a whole shot. Well, we awaited that solution of the matter with the cheerful resignation to which I have alluded. But the Master had some philosophy, too. "Huh!" said he, scornfully, as he got into position for the pitch, "Anyway, no duffer could have driven in here."

That has always seemed to me the last word in the philosophy of golf. All is, so far as one can see, everlastingly lost. The situation is beyond repair. Waterloo is rolling up its predestined battalions. Blucher* is not twenty miles away; he is just turning the corner. But you snatch a modicum of solace from the jaws of defeat. I know this, if only from a single experience of my own at Garden City. There were eight of us in this match, the Reds and the Blues, two Reds and two Blues for each foursome. There was a pot to be played for and eke+ a dinner. Nothing thrilling occurred in my foursome until we reached the home hole, the short hole over a pond. I drove a ball there which would have been ideal save for the detail that it came to rest in the shallows about two feet from the opposite shore. However, be kind enough to keep that ball in mind.

---

* Prussian General who, with Wellington, defeated Napoleon at Waterloo.
+ As in "eke out."

I drove another. And another. I dare say I might be driving them yet, but it was suddenly proposed—perhaps as a daylight-saving measure—and urged by the two Reds as well as by my fellow Blue, that I go over and play the first ball. I did so, stepping valiantly into the water, and with a niblick heaved the ball onto the green, near the cup, then sinking it for a three, and thereby, as it happened, winning the match, the dinner, and the pot. But stay! What do you suppose the Reds were doing, by that time all four of them gathered on the green? They were talking about rules, of course, even the two caitiff* Reds who in my foursome had suggested my playing the wet ball, which suggestion amounted, by all the unwritten laws of sportsmanship, to cancellation of any doggone rule. Ultimately, I am constrained to add, the rules had it. The Reds got the pot and the dinner. But did they get a shot out of the water, a good, respectable carry, to within a yard of the hole? Did they get a three? They did not. And I did. Not all the constitu-

---

* Cowardly.

tional law in the world could take the essence of the matter from me. Once more the philosophy of golf had come to the rescue. A good shot is a good shot, no matter how it penalizes you. If you can't get that consolation out of the game, then, pray, what can you get?

On Making a Hole in One

THE distinctive thing about it is that it has, in a sense, nothing to do with golf. That is to say, it is not a planned achievement, like driving a green, or getting successfully out of a bunker, or making a hole in three, or even in two. Making a hole in one is not an achievement at all, but an experience, such as falling in love. He would be a very stalwart fabulist who, having pitched his ball into the cup on a short hole, stood up and, without batting an eye, maintained that that was what he had aimed to do. There is the classical story of the duffer who holed out on a long drive and said, "I was afraid it wasn't going in." But that proves nothing save the ingenuity which goes to the making of golf-lore.

Making a hole in one, which, as I have said, has nothing to do with golf, is nevertheless one of the most sustaining stimuli known to golf-ers. It belongs to the metaphysical side of the game, among what George Meredith somewhere calls "the fine shades."[*] It is the equivalent in golf to that axiom in life at large: "Man never is, but always to be, blest."[+] Who that has gripped a mashie in his hand before a hole anywhere from one hundred and twenty-five to one hundred and seventy-five yards can maintain that he has never hoped in the bottom of his soul to reach the bottom of the cup? I dare swear that there isn't a short hole in the country which is not in-fested with the ghosts of these unspoken aspira-tions. I won't say that the wish is always there. But no golfer can truthfully assert that it has al-ways been a stranger to him.

It is done on some courses every season, yet it is never commonplace, and for some occult reason one rarely meets the man who did it; one gets the legend, almost invariably, at second or

---

[*] Meredith was a Victorian novelist; "fine shades" figures prominently in Meredith's novel *Sandra Belloni*.
[+] Alexander Pope's *Essay on Man*.

third hand. The connoisseur in these matters remembers, too, that there are distinctions hedging the thing about in such wise that a man may make a hole in one and yet lay no flattering unction to his soul. For example, though the essence of triumph here is luck, accident, there is a kind of accident which practically cancels the lucky shot. I have known a ball to be driven beyond the green against a tree, rebounding and then trickling into the cup. That was not the canonical mode of making a hole in one; it was crude, grossly fortuitous, helpful to the player's score, but in the nature of things depriving him of any lasting gusto.

I once made an approach shot which was a full five yards to the left of the green. A robin rose up just then, caught the ball on the small of his back, and with an indignant ruffle of his wings caused the ball to ricochet to within a yard or two of the pin. I call that an ornithological fluke, not a shot. Similarly, a player who whangs his ball against a tree or a rock and bounces it into the cup is automatically barred from claiming anything. What was he doing assailing the landscape?

The perfect shot that makes a hole in one is naturally not one that is all wrong to begin with; it is the shot that implies skill in that it reaches the green somewhere near the pin, demonstrating reasonable control over distance and direction. That is a good shot, anyway. The player may plume himself. But the life of our ideal shot is a dual life; luck revives it where skill leaves off. The moment of transition is the one in which your heart is literally in your mouth. To make a flawless pitch, to see your ball descending in the neighborhood of the pin, to watch it hit the green, say, six inches away! Has it dropped dead or is there a little roll left in it, and will luck follow through? There is nothing on earth quite like that moment of breathless suspense. I have known it, and I wouldn't trade it for anything in this world save a working bunker exit.

I once saw Jim Whigham* make a hole in one, on the short seventeenth, at Piping Rock,

---

* aka: H. J. Whigham, won the U.S. Amateur in 1896 and 1897.

and I shall never forget it. We were in a foursome, completely happy and quite unconscious of the fact that, in the phrase of Mr. H. G. Wells, "there are other dreams."[+] Suddenly the world was transformed. Jim pitched a consummate ball, clean as an orchid. It landed perhaps six feet from the pin, and then, like a startled mouse, ran into the cup. There was silence for a moment, followed by outcries. Yes, outcries. We must have fluttered the gulls at Montauk Point. I was interested in our hero's demeanor. It did not obviously alter. He is too good a sportsman to brag. But there stole over his Roman phiz[#] an indescribable glow. So might a man look who has just been told that they have reserved a tomb for him in Westminster Abbey. With a touch, just a touch, of the look that a conjurer wears when he takes a rabbit out of a hat. Jim has gone about ever since with his wonted calm. But, privately, I think he is a changed man.

[+] Wells was a famous English writer, mostly of science fiction. "There are other dreams" appears in Wells's *Sea Lady,* 1902.

[#] Chiefly British, from "physiognomy," meaning "face" or "expression."

And think, gentle reader, it might happen to anybody! To you. To me. For the prodigious appeal of this sublime coup is that it is not, I repeat, dependent upon proficiency in the game. It is as likely to happen to the duffer as to the star. A golfer may find it as impossible to get on a five-hundred-yard hole in two as it is for him to go back and fire the Ephesian dome, where a player like Barnes†† could make it with ease; but the same golfer may tackle one hundred and thirty-five yards with a mashie and see his ball hole out like a gentleman. On that emprise* he and the pro are on equal terms, though on every other count they are as far apart as the poles. Is there any other game which holds out anything like the same possibility? I have not, that I remember, ever made a hole in one.

---

†† Jim "Long Jim" Barnes, as his nickname indicates, was a big hitter. He won four majors from 1916 to 1925.
* A chivalrous adventure.

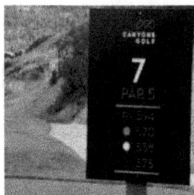

On Professionalism

IN the summer of 1922, the horizon was darkened by flocks of champions. Epical combats cheered the sportsman's heart. Yet, in the sporting world, at the very spots which should have been most exhilarating, the times got out of joint. "Babe" Ruth, they said, was suffering from a dislocation of his ego. Over at Wimbledon, Mdlle. Lenglen and Mrs. Mallory* were believed to be approaching one another in a mood inferred to be—well, just too sweet for anything. Mr. Dempsey,+ looking around for someone to

---

* Molly Mallory was America's best female tennis player in the 1920s. Susan Lenglen was French and was the best female tennis player in the world in the 1920s. They didn't like each other. Lenglen's lifetime match record was 341–7(!). She was as flamboyant and famous as she was dominant.
+ Jack Dempsey was boxing's heavyweight champion from 1919 to 1926.

stroke on the point of the jaw, would presently seem to be entangled with his own chancellery, and the next thing we would hear, his latest prospective victim had gone out of print. The affairs of golf alone sustained unruffled the even tenor of their way. What was the matter? Commentators on the "Babe" said it was temperament. I thought they were mistaken. It was something else, the insidious growth of which I have been watching for years. It was professionalism.

No, reader, I don't mean what perhaps you think I do. I don't mean the difference between the sportsman who is paid for his services and the sportsman who is not. I mean a fundamental difference between two points of view, between two ways of playing the game. There is a profound lesson in the remark of a certain novelist who produced some years ago one of the most brilliant historical romances of his time. He outlined the plot for me while it was in the making, described his hero and heroine, told me what they were to do, and promised that their hearts would fairly bleed through the narrative.

"All this will happen," he wrote, "if, under heaven, I can go on writing, like Thackeray,* as an amateur." He knew the perils of the—supposedly—impeccable "practised hand." He knew how easy it is for the maker of literature to become too infernally literary. He knew that the only safety lay in keeping the bloom of freshness on the rose. It is so in letters. It is so in art. It is the painter who takes out a patent on a type of picture and manufactures it by the gross who dies unlamented. He gets professionalized, which is to say that he exercises his facilities too much in accordance with what is expected of him. He develops, often, a consummate technic, but it is not unlike that of a trained seal; there is skill in it, but not exactly inspiration.

What has all this got to do with sport? Everything. It bears upon the point of view. There is a trite question which is rarely directed at anybody without an inflection indicating that there can be but one rational answer. The ques-

---

* William Makepeace Thackeray, 19th-century British novelist.

tion is: "Don't you play the game to win?" I wouldn't dream of answering in the negative. Of course one plays the game to win. But let us listen to old Montaigne on this subject. Discoursing on "how one ought to governe his will," he says:

> Consider how in meere vaine and frivolous actions, as at chesse, tennis and such like sports, this earnest and violent engaging with an ambitious desire to winne, doth presently cast both mind and limmes into disorder and indiscretion. Wherein a man doth both dazle his sight and distemper his whole body. Hee who demeaneth himselfe with most moderation both in winning and loosing, is ever neerest unto him selfe, and hath his wits best about him. The lesse he is moved or passionate in play, the more safely doth he governe the same, and to his greater advantage. We hinder the mind's seazure and holdfast,

by giving her so many things to seize upon.*

Suppose we ask that ancient question in another form: "Do you aim at perfection or success?" Golf answers as no other sport can. In baseball, in tennis, in the prize-ring, in any game that brings two players face to face, you've got to win; winning is the essence of the game. This is in the nature of things. The technic of the racket, I take it, has its beauties, but it is the instrument of a rivalry so close and personal that it cannot humanly be separated in its employment from the ambition to succeed. Where better could we look for proof than at the top of the game? Consider the match which drew the eyes of the sporting world to Wimbledon. Those two ladies are admittedly the queens of the court. What was the upshot of their conflict to be? Nominally, to demonstrate that one more than the other represented the perfection of tennis. But I take the liberty of having some doubts. I dare swear

---

* From *Essays*, by Michel de Montaigne, who, during the late 16th century, established the essay as a literary form.

that what Mdlle. Lenglen achieved was, first and last, success, a triumph, and that that was all that interested the world.

Now, consider the difference in golf. Hagen came back, praise be, a winner. But look at the scores and ask if there were no other laurels. They were all over the place, and I maintain that that was what made the Battle of Sandwich thrilling.[+] They were so abundant for no other reason than that golf is a striving after perfection, a struggle in which each individual shot has its status, its interest. Again, it is in the nature of things, and again we glance at that little matter of professionalism. The course was crowded with "pros," with stars, men who make their living by golf, and they all played to win; yet, paradoxically, while they so played, the genius of the game still kept their eyes glued on nothing but an ideal of perfection. Grantland Rice, who knows, is forever noting the moral poise of this or that master of the game. He shows us men like Ha-

---

[+] Walter Hagen won the (British) Open Championship in 1922 at Royal St. George's in Sandwich, England—the first American to do so, beating runners-up Jim Barnes & George Duncan.

gen and Barnes going devotedly after the crown but playing each stroke as a painter might lay on his brush. He speaks of their competitive ardor. But always, with them, there comes first the rigor of the game, the calm, well-considered making of the shot. How can it be brought off so well if the mind is fretted by external things?

I have observed, in one of the commonest of a golfer's foibles, the effect of a variance between the grasp at perfection and the grasp at success. Two players separate at the tee and meet on the green with, say, a ten-foot putt and a six-foot putt to make, neither knowing the state of the other's score on that hole. The man who is away sinks his putt. "What was that?" says his opponent, and, on learning how hard pressed he is, remarks defiantly: "Well, I've got to sink this for a half." Tense with anxiety, he misses his putt and loses the hole. He would have had a better chance, I think, if he had kept his mouth shut, for then he would have been thinking only of the putt. When he finds out what he has to match or beat, he gains, if you like, an added incentive, but he also takes on a handicap.

Professionalism, in short, does not consist in taking pay; it consists in doubling a sport with an irrelevant preoccupation. It is the confusion of an art with its reward, whether the latter be cash, applause, or the champion's insignia. It is the degradation of technic to an end foreign to its spirit. It tinctures all games, and I would not pretend that it has left golf utterly untouched. But in golf its chances of working evil are slighter, because its antidote is more obviously and potently present. Let the reader who questions this test it for himself. Let him observe how he is affected by his various clubs from tee to green; how the driver, the brassie*, the iron, the putter, each in its turn confronts him with a problem and lures him into endless study. What is it that absorbs him, demanding all his attention—his own shots or his opponent's, the game itself or the score that is piling up, success or perfection? Is not his hope of the one dependent on his approximation to the other? Of one thing I am

---

* Somewhere between today's driver and a 3-wood.

sure—if he is blind to the distinction involved, it will be revealed, infallibly, in his score.

On the Devil in Golf

IF the devil is perfectly at home on a golf-course it is doubtless because that place is so thoroughly well paved with good intentions. There can be no question as to his presence there. How, otherwise, are you to account for certain things that happen to golfers? Surely it is not "the spirits of the wise" that do "sit in the clouds and mock us."* It is a dark and sinister force, and, so far from being content to perch upon a cloud, it comes right down to earth, infests every turn of the course, and even lurks in the locker-room. If you do not believe this, accept an invitation to play in a foursome at a club you have never visited before. Let it be on a Saturday, when the crowd is thickest and the time-card is as adamant. Linger a little longer over

---

* Shakespeare, *Henry IV, Part Two.*

luncheon than you should and then hurry to dress. Look out of the window and observe the throng at the first tee. Look at your watch and bend to tie your shoe with the realization that you have just two minutes in which to take your place in the game. And then have your shoe-lace snap, close to the eyelet. I will not repeat your gloss upon this pretty situation.

> 'Tis not mine to record
> What Angels shrink from: even the very Devil
> On this occasion his own work abhorred.[+]

And no wonder. I would not make a mountain out of a mole-hill, a life-line out of a shoe-lace. Goodness knows that, though men have died and the worms have eaten them, it has not been because they were late at the first tee. But it is the kind of mischance that makes you "dancing mad," and it is unthinkable without diabolical intervention.

[+] Lord Byron, *The Vision of Judgment.*

There is a whole catalogue of these little pin pricks which are to be credited to his majesty. Take your short-sighted man, who can't play without his golf glasses. Let him discover, on some such visit as I have indicated, that he has remembered to bring everything else but has left the one indispensable aid at home. Reader, did you ever try playing golf with a pair of bifocals on your nose? If not, try it, and then say whether your predicament is devilish or not. I know of only one other posture of affairs to beat it. That is to reach, say, the tenth hole, well out on the course, remote from the club-house, a good "twelve miles from a lemon,"* and to take out on that sequestered spot the cigar you have been saving up for about the middle of the game. Everybody in the foursome is in the same blissful case. Pipes come out, and cigarettes. Everybody is ready to light up. And there isn't a match in the house! Not one of the players has a match. Not one of the caddies has a match. There isn't a man with a match anywhere in sight, for miles

---

* From Sydney Smith, much-quoted 19th-century English cler-gyman and wit.

around. For once Lucifer belies his name. You call upon it in vain. He has gone up a tree to mock at you. Positively, at a moment like that, I have heard his derisive chuckle.

It is when the game moves on that he comes down and moves with it. You can almost see him. His gloomy features, "like a midnight dial, Scowl the dark index of a fearful hour."[*] It is the hour, known to every golfer, in which you try to repeat. Then ensues diabolism of an uncannily high order. You made the hole, a day earlier in the week, in par. You know just how you did it. So much distance is to be assigned to your drive. The second shot will leave you, inevitably, with an easy approach. You have hopes of a four. You are certain of a five. The devil is most like himself at such a juncture. He lets you have your drive, thereby increasing your certitude. He is good to your second shot. But although you know all about the approach, just

---

[*] Thomas Lovell Beddoes, 19th-century poet and playwright.

why you should "go easy" with it, just why you should avoid running over, he comes nimbly to the front and takes you into the pit beyond. O pit, pit, how aptly art thou named! Art thou not his designated dwelling-place? It is there, above all other hazards, that you are "as helpless as the Devil can wish."[+]

You land there never so decisively, never so snugly ensconced in an unplayable lie, as when, having won the hole once, you try to repeat. I can't believe that it is pure error that accounts for this special brand of humiliation. Some analysts lay it to self-consciousness. It is just because you are thinking of repeating, they say, that you lose your grip on concentration and fetch up on toast. It is the demon, rather, who works the evil. One of my fellow golfers is a particularly good driver, straight and far. In a recent game I saw him slice his ball out of bounds from nearly every tee, sometimes two balls from the

---

[+] Lord Byron, *The Vision of Judgment.*

same tee. He knew better, and there were several players present quite willing to tell him the reason for it if he needed light. But he couldn't help going on slicing. He kept at it with the devotion of a train-dispatcher. He knew nothing about my theory of demoniacal possession, yet I was not in the least surprised when he laid it all on the devil.

Some students of the game, strangers to the delights of mystical speculation, are prone to explain away the more fantastic of golfing collapses by what they call, with scientific simplicity and aplomb, "physical condition." It is all a matter of nerves, they tell you, a matter of coordination. As a friend of mine remarked the other day, "the character of the drive is determined by the synchronization of the pathway of the hands and the pathway of the club-head at the moment of impact," and this in turn depends upon your bodily state. Can't you hear that chuckle coming up from the pit? As a matter of fact, there is nothing like the complete disequilibrium of all your corporeal faculties to assure you one of the best of your games. It is when you are outrageously fit that you fall by the wayside. Get

up in the morning feeling like a king, all set for a
game that you have long been anticipating. Go
to the course in the most luxurious of cars. Drive
off in cloudless weather, with a cherished friend,
having a clear field ahead and no one to press
you. It is a million dollars to a tin doughnut that
you will flub your drive. It is when all these conditions are reversed and you are made aware,
with the upward swing of your club, that you've
got a nail in your shoe, that you really hit the ball.
Look at the champions, with their not infrequent
"slumps." Is it physical condition that betrays
them? Why, they haven't any nerves. It is a sub-
tler enemy that lays them low. The devil, after all,
is more respectable to cite than an alibi, the most
hateful pest in golf. When a great golfer misses a
fifteen-inch putt, let him repeat for his consolation the words of Cassio: "Every inordinate cup
is unbless'd, and the ingredient is a devil."*

---

* Shakespeare's *Othello*.

On Dufferdom

IT is a broad and goodly land, this land of dufferdom, its limits marked only by those of the golf-courses of the earth. Does not its representative figure deserve some consideration? Voltaire* would appear to have answered that question as far back as the eighteenth century. To the duffer, who reminded him that even duffers must exist, he sweetly replied: "I don't see the necessity." There are commentators who stand by that assertion to this day. They are a little too austere. After all, the duffer is a friendly human brother. Suppose he does top his ball. Nevertheless, hath not a duffer "hands, organs, dimensions, senses, affections, passions"?+ He abounds in error, of course. Mayhap he is fairly steeped in it. But—

---

* 18th-century French writer, philosopher, and wit.
+ Shakespeare's *The Merchant of Venice.*

"Errors, like straws, upon the surface flow; He who would search for pearls must dive below."#

Let us then dive into dufferdom, an adventure which especially appeals to me at the moment, for as I write the welkin§ is ringing with the exploits of Mr. Jesse Sweetser,± winner of the national amateur championship at Brookline. His scores read like the "Eroica."* The talk is all of birdies and eagles. If one listens to it long enough, one develops the suspicion that golf has been lifted to a Homeric plane and that only Homeric men are fit to play it. But the duffer remains—immovable, monumental. We may turn to him, if only in the spirit of Calverley+ and his invocation to that "grinder who serenely grindest":

> 'Tis not that thy mien is stately,
> 'Tis not that thy tones are soft;

John Dryden's play, *All for Love*, 1677.
§ The sky or heaven.
± Won the 1922 U.S. Amateur Championship.
* Presumably, Beethoven's *Symphony No. 3.*
+ Charles Stuart Calverley, 19th-century poet and wit.

'Tis not that I care so greatly
For the same thing played so oft:
But I've heard mankind abuse thee;
And perhaps it's rather strange,
But I thought that I would choose thee
For encomium, as a change."#

I thought sympathetically of the duffer not long since, in the midst of a conversation which seemed to leave him no excuse for being at all. The merits of a certain hole had come up for discussion. It was a hard hole, so hard as to be denounced by some as merely tricky and demoralizing. When I had the chance, I submitted the problem to the one august authority in these matters, the wizard and wonder-worker, Mr. Charles MacDonald.* He settled it in a saying which I suppose might well be inscribed in letters of gold over the portal of every golf-club. "Well," quoth he, "a golf-course is designed for men who

---

Lines on Hearing the Organ [Grinder], 1872.
* Winner of the first U.S. Amateur in 1895, he also laid out the first 18-hole course in America. The World Golf Hall of Fame states that Macdonald "can justly be called the 'Father of American golf.'"

can play golf." How everlastingly true and inspiring that is! It sums up the rigor and the glory of the game. It erects the only authentic standard. To question it would be to speak disrespectfully of the equator. Your golf-course is unquestionably made for the men who can play golf. But, on the other hand, if one may with diffidence hazard a small interrogation: Who on earth keeps it going?

Establish yourself comfortably on the bench at the first tee and watch one foursome after another drive off. Keep careful tally for an hour or so. Then tot up the numbers of those who played golf and the numbers of those who launched themselves blithely into dufferdom. The latter region has, I verily believe, a density of population rivaling that of a Chinese slum. Only, you see, there is nothing in the least slummy about it. On the contrary, its sunny slopes are rich in elbow-room, which is used in ecstasy by happy myriads. Not for them the sublime certainty of a Sweetser. In Grantland Rice's account of that young old master's dazzling triumph, I find this tribute to his flawless form: "He reminded you of a well-oiled machine that could continue to send the ball on a straight line for year after year, until the cogs wore out." The duffer's straight line may be, in a sense, an annual affair, but there is otherwise nothing of the inerrant machine about him. He hasn't a cog to his name. But, I ask again, is it the Sweetsers of this world who keep a golf-course going?

What a deadly place a golf-course would be if they did! It might please a Henry Ford to watch the functioning of a long procession of well-oiled machines, and the rest of us would, for a time at least, be so keen about the spectacle that the committee would probably have to cover up the rough with bleachers. But sooner or later the duffer would rebel. He would be first fascinated, then stupefied, and, finally, bored to death. He would want the feel of a club in his hand. For a little while he would shrink from the ordeal of making a birdie whether he liked it or not. He would end by making that hole in seven and glorying in his shame. Driven to bay by an irate committee, he would ask the members if they would not, for one thing, look at the statistics. What these would reveal in the personnel of almost any club I have already hinted. And there are other items that build up a formidable economic total. Who is it that buys and tries every new club? The duffer. Who is it that buys and tries every new ball? The duffer. Who is that who enters sweepstakes after sweepstakes, counting his defeats as naught? The duffer. And so on. He is the rock-ribbed foundation of golf. If he were to withdraw, the golf-courses of the country would infallibly bust up. But I would not dwell importunately on his status as an economic factor. Indeed, I would far rather emphasize his traits as a sportsman, his significance as an embodiment of the immortal spirit of the game.

The duffer is nothing if not an artist. To quote my friend Rice* again: "In golf there is no man who is ever master of his destiny." That is the artist's point of view. The duffer has it, re-

---

* Grantland Rice also worked at the *New York Tribune*.

joices in it, and is steadily faithful to it. For him the very mutability of the game constitutes one of its strongest lures. He faces each game as an experiment, just as a painter faces a new canvas. The thing may prove a botch. It may prove a jewel. And this artistic conception of the struggle involves a peculiarly exquisite satisfaction in victory, when the victory comes off. Rarity, most of us will admit, is one of the supreme blisses of life. The passion for it is a universal attribute of human nature. There are few men who would not exchange a fixed income for a thumping windfall. It must be, beyond all peradventure, a delectable thing to play six holes in succession in authoritative, automatic par, to play them with the assurance of an acrobat sailing over six elephants at a jump. But, frankly, can this trained, rehearsed achievement equal in high emotion the unexpected prowess of the duffer who makes a two where he never made a two before? The question answers itself. It is like painting a composition that has always got confused and suddenly having it resolve itself into perfect clarity.

Think of the moments in a duffer's pro-
gress in which he perceives that it really is pro-
gress that he is making. He studies Sarazen's grip
until he feels like Laocoon[‡‡] in the coils of the
serpents, but some fine morning he actually gets
the hang of it. He wrestles with his brassie in
despair, and then, unaccountably, discovers that
it is the best club in his bag, the one with which
he can do incredible things. He makes a two-shot
hole out of an interminable brute that had pre-
viously done nothing but deface his score. And,
mark you, he does all this by the process which is
the very life-blood of the game, by the process of
trying. I never could comprehend the compla-
cent scorn of the Pharisee in golf for the duffer
at whom he directs his gibes. When the potentate
misses a two-foot putt it is, I suppose, because
the solar system shifted just then. The duffer in
the same case is assumed to have sounded the
depths of ineptitude and receives the opprobri-
um due to personal guilt. I have seen numbers of
very good players do fairly terrible things. We

[‡‡] Greek mythological priest/seer crushed to death by serpents.

read about them even in historic matches. No-body is blamed for them. Neither should the duffer be blamed. What he needs is not blame but sympathy.

If he deserves it for anything, it is for the all-essential virtue which he shares with the elect, the virtue of resolution. You couldn't dampen his ardor with a cloudburst. Sweetser, Hagen, Sarazen, Ouimet,* and the rest fight on through thick and thin. So does the duffer. That is where he is on all fours with the best of them, though his resources, compared with theirs, are like windblown sparks compared with the roaring flame at the heart of a conflagration. He may top his ball, as I have said before, but he will tackle it again, and again, and yet again. His head is bloody but unbowed. Jocund as the morning, after unnumbered rebuffs, he swings his driver from the first tee and with Gilbert[+] sings:

---

[*] Francis Ouimet, as an amateur, won the 1913 U.S. Open.
[+] W. S. Gilbert. 19th-century writer; with Arthur Sullivan created *HMS Pinafore, The Mikado,* and other comic operas.

Roll on, thou ball, roll on!
Through pathless realms of Space
Roll on!
What though I'm in a sorry case?
What though I cannot meet my bills?
What though I suffer toothache's ills?
What though I swallow countless pills?
Never you mind!
Roll on!